Contents

Learning to walk

When you were a baby, all you could do was wriggle and roll, but you soon learnt how to crawl.

Then you learnt to balance on your feet, and before long you were walking.

8

Your strong legs have joints
at your ankles, knees and hips.
Muscles control the way these
joints bend.

You can walk, dance, run and do
all kinds of physical activities.

9

Slithering and sliding

Some animals have no arms or legs. They get about by slithering and sliding.

When snakes wriggle along they move sideways.

When snails move they shuffle their bodies on a mat of slime which leaves a trail behind them.

Two legs

Birds have two legs the same as people. Some have long legs for wading in water. Others have webs between their toes for swimming.

Birds' feet have three long toes pointing forwards and one pointing backwards. With these they can perch easily on twigs and branches.

How many toes do you have?

Many animals have four legs—but they don't have any arms or wings.

14

Many four-legged animals move at great speed on long slender legs. They run much faster than people.

Others move more slowly because their legs are shorter or their bodies heavier.

Hooves and paws

Some animals have hooves which are hard like your toe nails. Each foot may have a single hoof or it may be split into two or four.

Other animals have paws. Their toes are round and soft and have pads underneath like cushions. Each toe has a claw at the end.

What sort of toes do the tortoise and the chameleon have?

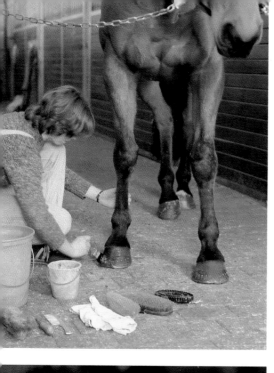

Six legs or more

The spider has eight legs and a pair of feelers. The crab has eight legs and a pair of pincers with claws.

The caterpillar has three pairs of legs and five pairs of suckers.

The millipede has many legs.

Can you find these animals and their legs in the pictures?

19

Butterflies have two pairs of wings. These move separately to control their flight.

Birds have one pair of wings and a tail. They can spread their feathers to help them fly.

Great swimmers

Animals with flippers are slow and clumsy on land but when they dive into water they are swift and powerful swimmers.

Can you swim?

Do you think you can swim
as fast as the seal?

23

Underwater creatures

Fish spend all their lives under water. They swim by waggling their tails and steer with their fins.

Some underwater creatures are mammals. They need to come up to the surface to breathe air.

Do you know how fish breathe?

Travelling anywhere

People can travel through the air like birds and under the sea like fish.

They do this by using special equipment.

What other equipment or vehicles do people make to help them travel across the world?

Useful words

birds Warm-blooded animals with two legs and two wings. They usually fly and hop or walk when on the ground. Some have webbed feet for paddling or swimming. A few, like penguins or ostriches, cannot fly.

fish Cold-blooded animals that live underwater and breathe through gills. They get about by waggling their tails and steering with their fins.

insects Small animals that usually have six legs and two or four wings for flying. Their bodies are divided into three parts.

mammals Warm-blooded animals that usually live on land and have two or four legs. Some, like whales, live underwater and swim like fish but breathe air at the surface. Some, like seals, live partly in water and partly on land. These mammals usually have flippers for swimming.

29

Index